How to be Brilliant at

RECORDING

IN HISTORY

Sue Lloyd

 Brilliant Publications

We hope you and your class enjoy using this book. Other books in the series include:

Science titles

How to be Brilliant at Recording in Science	1 897675 10 0
How to be Brilliant at Science Investigations	1 897675 11 9
How to be Brilliant at Electricity, Light & Sound	1 897675 13 5
How to be Brilliant at Materials	1 897675 12 7

English titles

How to be Brilliant at Writing Stories	1 897675 00 3
How to be Brilliant at Writing Poetry	1 897675 01 1
How to be Brilliant at Grammar	1 897675 02 X
How to be Brilliant at Making Books	1 897675 03 8
How to be Brilliant at Spelling	1 897675 08 9
How to be Brilliant at Reading	1 897675 09 7

Maths titles

How to be Brilliant at Using a Calculator	1 897675 04 6
How to be Brilliant at Algebra	1 897675 05 4
How to be Brilliant at Numbers	1 897675 06 2
How to be Brilliant at Shape and Space	1 897675 07 0
How to be Brilliant at Mental Arithmetic	1 897675 21 6

Geography title

How to be Brilliant at Recording in Geography	1 897675 31 3

If you would like further information on these or other titles published by Brilliant Publications, please write to the address given below.

Published by Brilliant Publications,
The Old School Yard, Leighton Road, Northall,
Dunstable, Bedfordshire LU6 2HA

Written by Sue Lloyd
Illustrated by Kate Ford
Cover photograph by Martyn Chillmaid

Printed in Malta by Interprint Ltd

© Sue Lloyd 1997
ISBN 1 897675 22 4

First published in 1997
Reprinted 1999, 2001
10 9 8 7 6 5 4 3

Contents

Introduction

How to be Brilliant at Recording in History contains 40 photocopiable worksheets designed to lead children through a range of historical skills. The sheets are divided into five sections which reflect the Key Elements of the National Curriculum:

- chronology
- historical knowledge and understanding
- interpretations of history
- historical enquiry
- organization and communication

The sheets have been arranged according to their main focus, but all the sheets cover skills from more than one Key Element. For example, page 10 (Changes in history) is in the Chronology section, but also uses skills from 'Historical knowledge and understanding' and 'Organization and communication'.

Most of the worksheets are self-explanatory, but we recommend that you read the teacher's notes before using the sheets. The notes will give you pointers and ideas for each sheet. These are only suggestions and there are many ways of adapting the material to suit the needs of individual children. All of the sheets are suitable for differentiated work and there are many suggestions for extension activities in the teacher's notes.

Using the worksheets

GETTING STARTED
Before I start   **page 7**
- assesses children's prior knowledge.

CHRONOLOGY
Building a timeline   **page 8**
- children can give each box a date, write or draw pictures in the boxes, then write the date on the timeline to the right;
- or number each box, then place the number on the timeline;
- more able children could summarize each box, give it a title, then write it on the timeline.

Stratigraphy   **page 9**
- stratigraphy shows what happened at different times in the past by looking at evidence in the ground;
- more able children could estimate the dates of the pieces of evidence.

Changes in history   **page 10**
- children can write or draw pictures in the boxes;
- suggested themes – clothes, transport, homes, leisure, weapons.

KNOWLEDGE AND UNDERSTANDING
Topic flower   **page 11**
- use at the end of a topic to assess children's knowledge and understanding;
- or use as a summing up exercise;
- suggested themes – place names, famous people or events, myths and legends, food, buildings.

Database – event   **page 12**
- information from this sheet can be transferred to a computer database;
- more able children could record the causes of the event.

Database – person   **page 13**
- information from this sheet can be transferred to a computer database;
- more able children could record the evidence used to complete the database.

People   **page 14**
- information can be transferred to a computer database;
- use fictitious people, eg a sailor, a tradesperson, an entertainer and a lord;
- or use real people, eg Elizabeth I, Walter Raleigh, Shakespeare and Thomas More.

Similarities and differences   **page 15**
- suggested comparisons – Anglo-Saxons and Vikings, town houses and country houses, life today and life in Egyptian times.

Comparing people from the past   **page 16**
- complements page 15;
- suggested comparisons – rich, middle class and poor;
- can be used for aspects of local history;
- the last column is blank for teachers to choose their own heading.

Postcard from the past   **page 17**
- can be used with any period in history.

A tour   **page 18**
- more able children could record the schedule.

Using my senses   **page 19**
- suggested locations – a town, church, battle, school, journey.

Reasons and results   **page 20**
- suggested issues – Roman invasion, voyages of exploration, poverty in Victorian towns.

In other places   **page 21**
- the last boxes are blank for teachers to choose their own headings;
- suggestions for the empty boxes – Rome, Spain, France, the New World.

Then and now   **page 22**
- more able children could explain *why* the greatest and least changes have taken place.

INTERPRETATIONS OF HISTORY
What people said   **page 23**
- use primary evidence, secondary evidence or both.

What people wrote   **page 24**
- use primary evidence, secondary evidence or both.

The Daily _____   **page 25**
- children can work in pairs, each writing a different viewpoint;
- or one child could write about two sequential events.

HISTORIC ENQUIRY

ORGANIZATION AND COMMUNICATION

Before I start

I am going to be learning about:

I think they looked like this…

I think they lived …

I think they liked…

I also know…

I got my information from …

I can check my information …

How to be Brilliant at Recording in History

Building a timeline

This timeline is about …

Date:

Date:

Date:

Date:

Date:

Date:

Date:

Date:

There are lots of ways to use this sheet.

Stratigraphy

I am looking at these pieces of evidence:

This is where the evidence might have come from:

	Twentieth century
	Victorian
	Tudor
	Viking
	Anglo-Saxon
	Roman

I can estimate the date of these pieces of evidence:

Evidence:	Evidence:	Evidence:
Date:	Date:	Date:

Changes in history

I am looking at changes in…

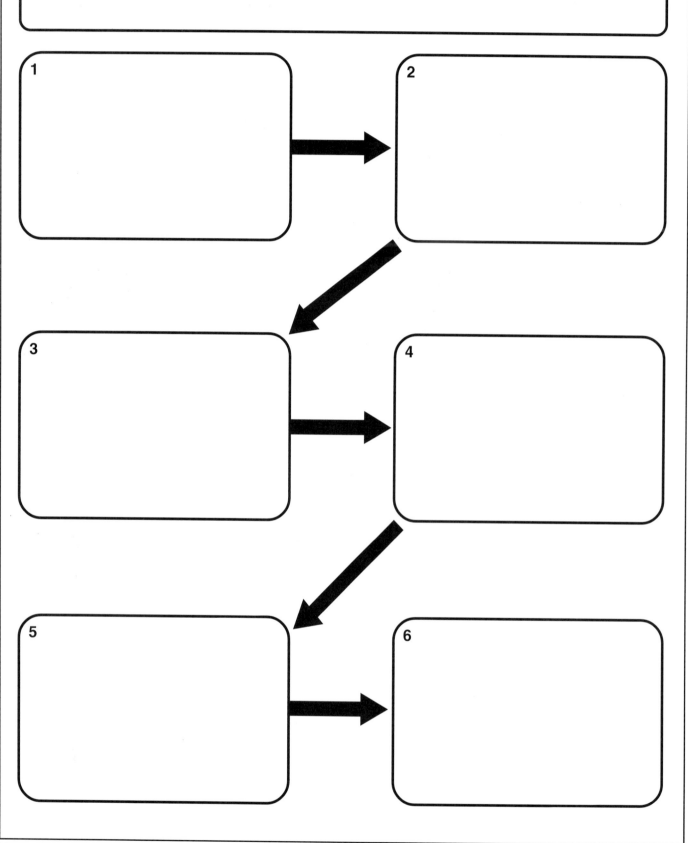

1

2

3

4

5

6

Topic flower

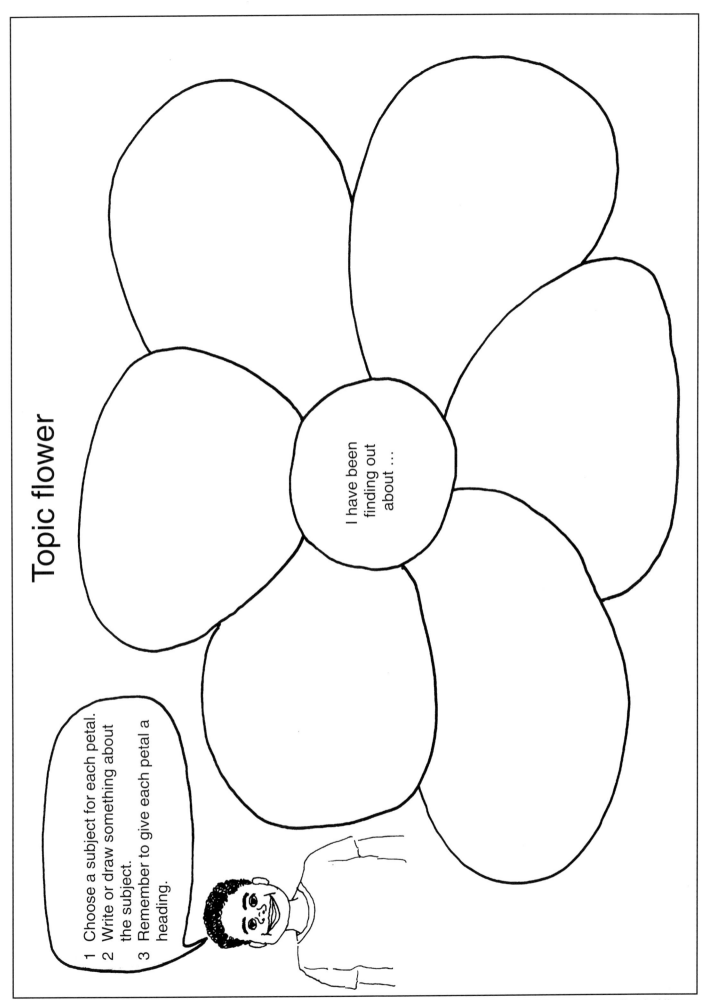

I have been finding out about …

1. Choose a subject for each petal.
2. Write or draw something about the subject.
3. Remember to give each petal a heading.

How to be Brilliant at Recording in History

11

Database – event

Event:

Date:

Place:

People:

What happened:

Causes:

You can use this information in lots of ways. For example:
- a TV or radio report
- a news item in a comic
- a newspaper report.

Database – person

	Evidence
Name:	
Description:	
Personality:	
Famous for:	
Other information:	
Sources:	

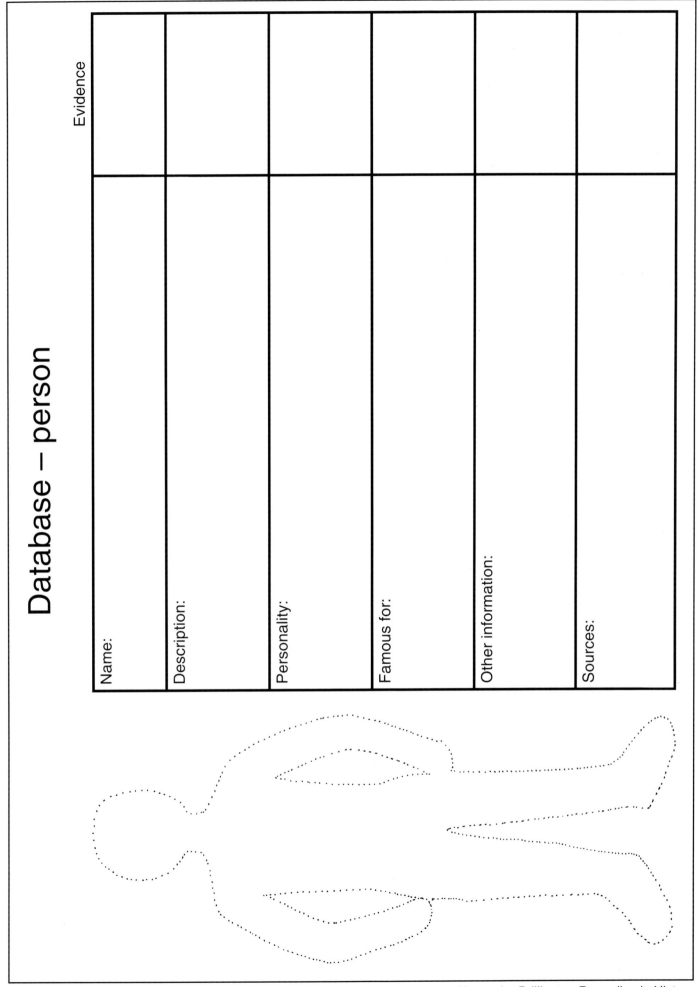

How to be Brilliant at Recording in History

People

My name is …

I am a …

The best part of
my life is …

The worst part
of my life is…

My name is …

I am a …

The best part
of my life is …

The worst part
of my life is…

My name is …

I am a …

The best part
of my life is …

The worst part
of my life is…

My name is …

I am a …

The best part
of my life is …

The worst part
of my life is…

Similarities and differences

I am comparing _____ with _____

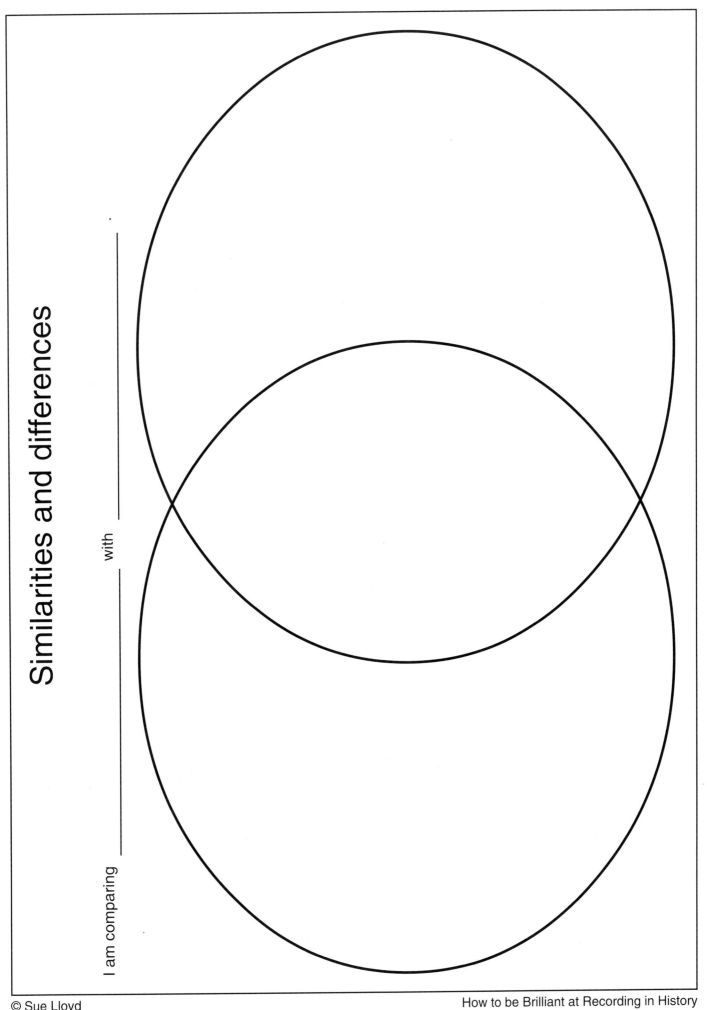

How to be Brilliant at Recording in History

Comparing people from the past

	Clothes	Food	Travel	Buildings	Religion

I used these sources:

A postcard from the past

I am sending a postcard from …

Dear

You could write about:
- the people you meet
- the places you visit
- the food
- the accommodation
- the scenery
- an interesting event
- the wildlife
- how you travel

How to be Brilliant at Recording in History

A tour

This is our schedule

Time	Destination

Welcome to a tour of …

Your guide's name is …

Here is a map of our route:

You may find this information useful:

We will visit:

Using my senses

If I travelled back in time …

I might see …

I might hear …

I might taste …

I might smell …

I might touch …

The best part of my trip would be …

How to be Brilliant at Recording in History

Reasons and results

I am finding out about …

causes

Brainstorm the reasons why your event happened.

consequences

Brainstorm the results of your event.

In other places

I have been finding out about …

This is what it was like in parts of …

England

Ireland

Scotland

Wales

How to be Brilliant at Recording in History

Then and now

I am looking at …

Then	**Now**

The greatest changes have been …

The least changes have been …

What people said

I am finding out about ...

This was said by

This was said by

This was said by

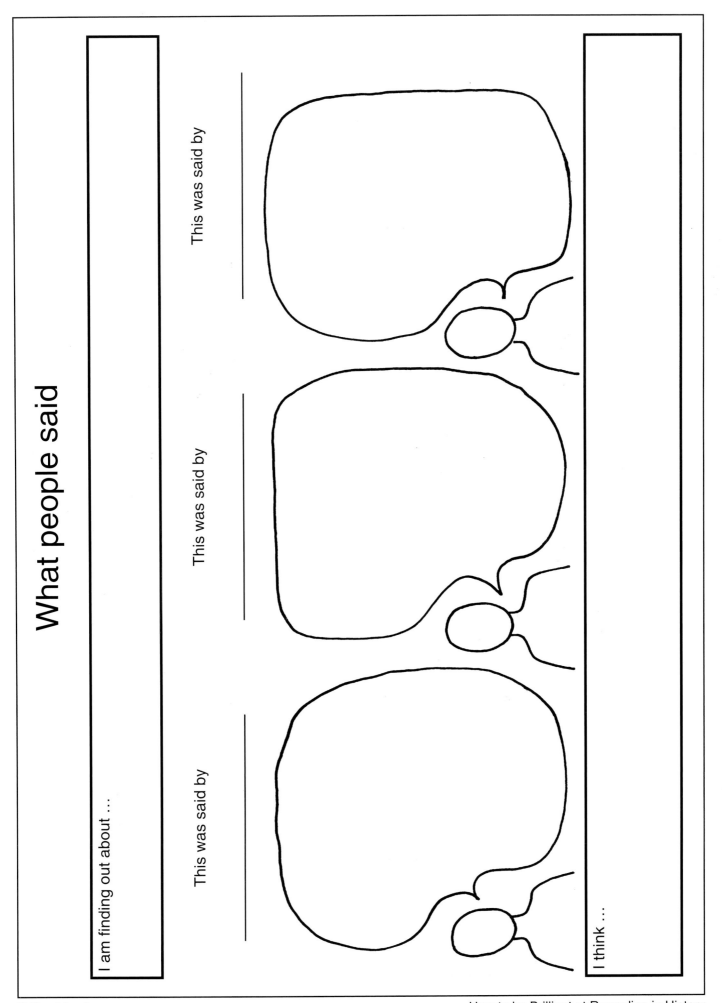

I think ...

How to be Brilliant at Recording in History

What people wrote

I am finding out about ....

This was written by

This was written by

This was written by

This was written by

This was written by

I think ...

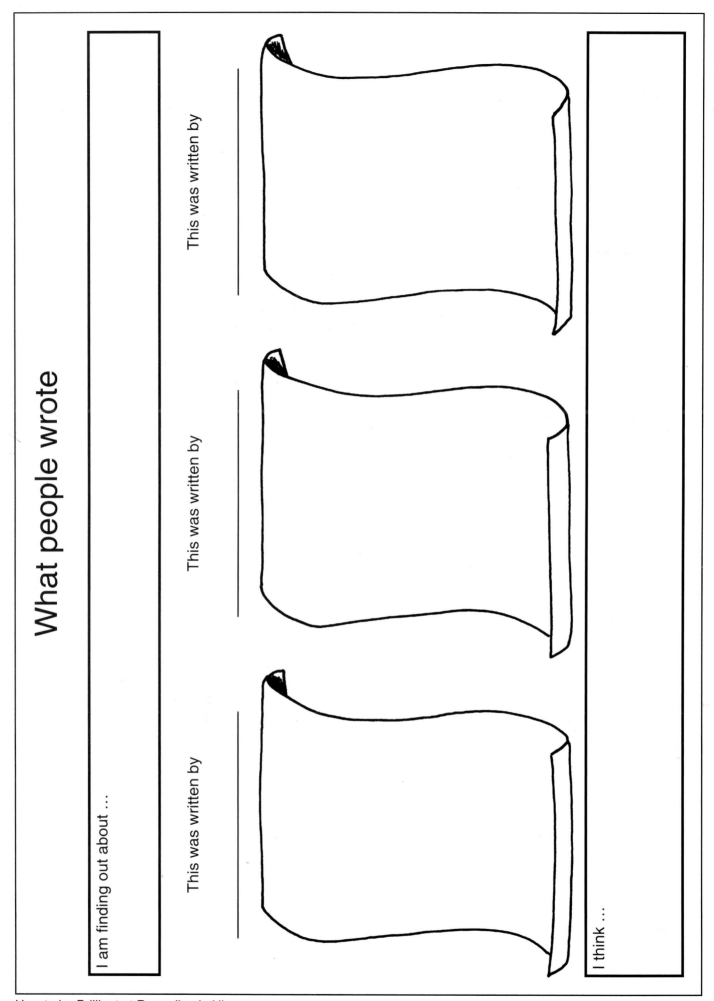

The Daily

Date

Reporter:

The Daily

Date

Reporter:

How to be Brilliant at Recording in History

Historical evidence

I am thinking about different kinds of historical evidence:

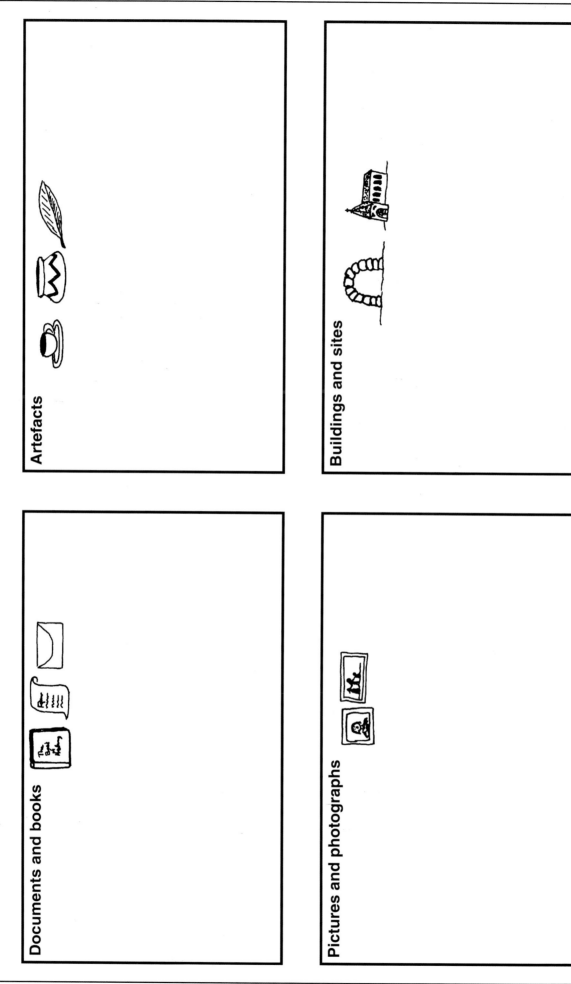

Documents and books

Artefacts

Pictures and photographs

Buildings and sites

Primary or secondary evidence?

I can sort evidence into sets:

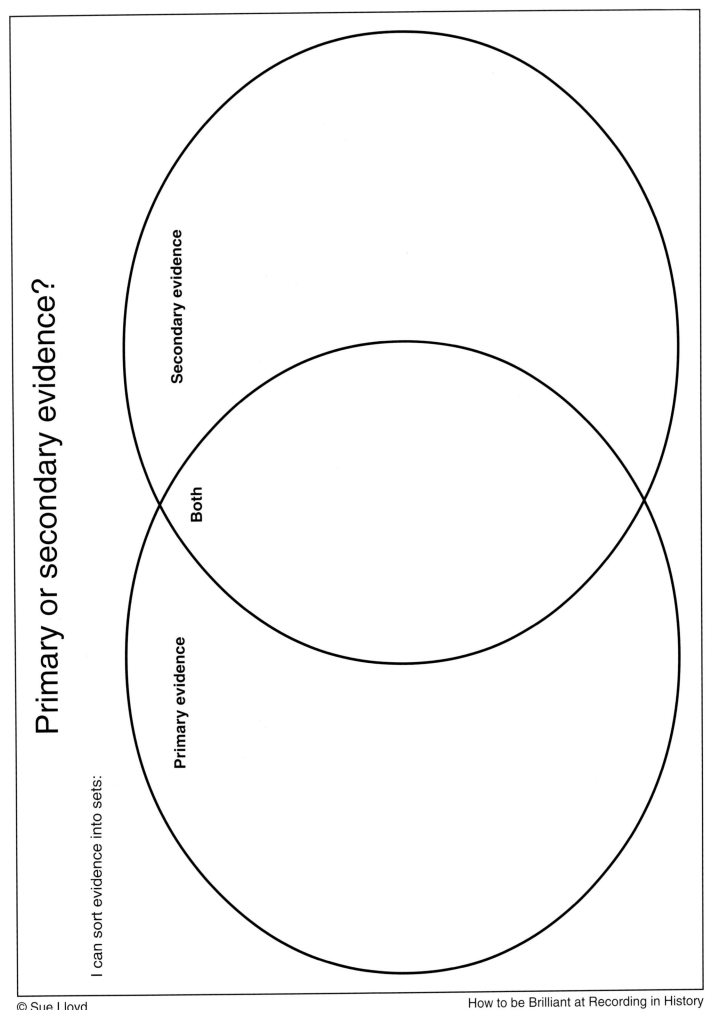

Secondary evidence

Both

Primary evidence

How to be Brilliant at Recording in History

Class museum

These artefacts are in the class museum.

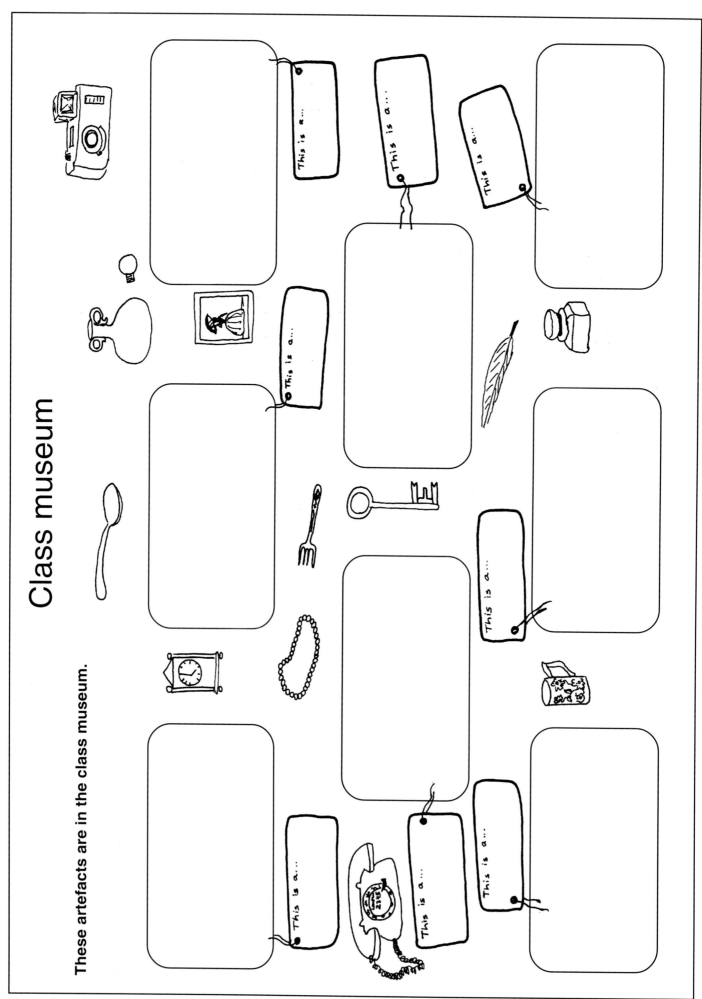

The tags read: "This is a...."

How to be Brilliant at Recording in History

The mystery object

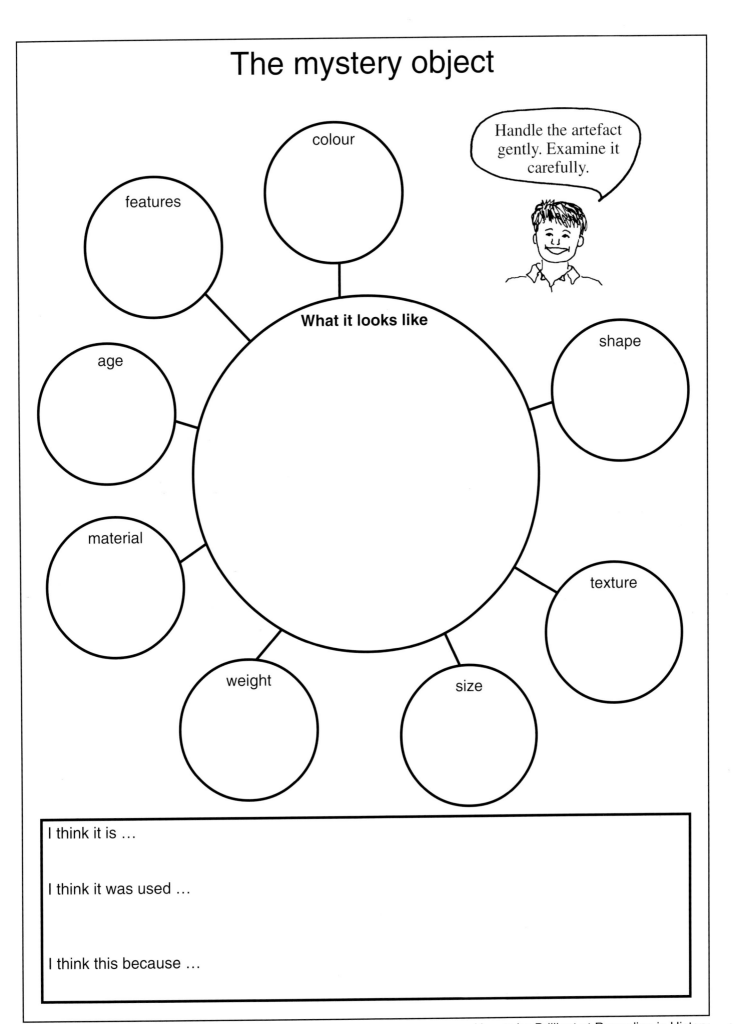

colour

features

Handle the artefact gently. Examine it carefully.

What it looks like

shape

age

material

texture

weight

size

I think it is …

I think it was used …

I think this because …

How to be Brilliant at Recording in History

Working with clues

I have looked at these clues:

Clue 1	Clue 2	Clue 3

Clue 1 tells me …

Clue 2 tells me …

Clue 3 tells me …

Historians use clues to help them build up a picture of what happened in the past.

After looking at the clues, I think that …

Clues are everywhere!

Clues are everywhere! You have to be alert to spot them!

Clue	Date I found it	Description	Age or date of clue	This clue tells me …

I can sort the clues into groups:

Time capsule, 1

This is what I would bury in my lunchbox time capsule.

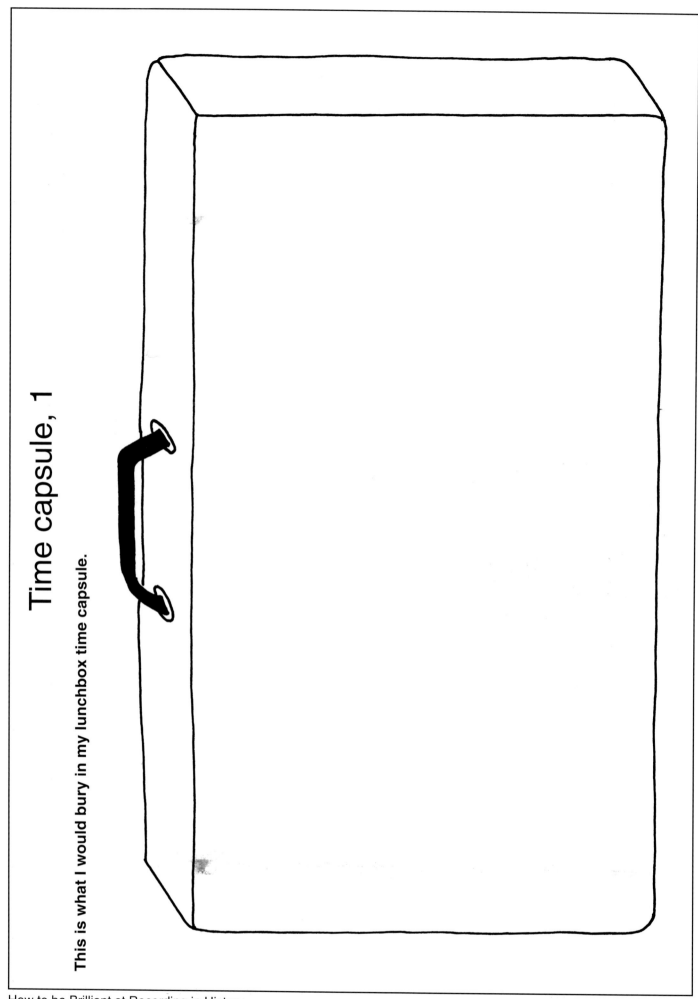

Time capsule, 2

This is what _____ **could have buried.**

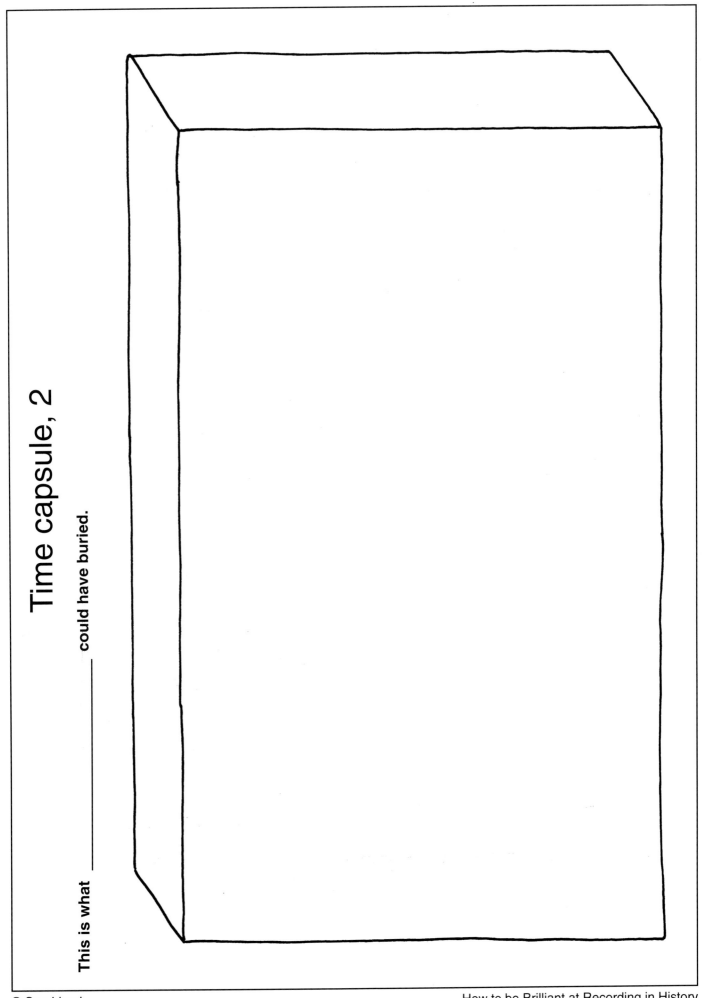

How to be Brilliant at Recording in History

Whose clue?

I am trying to find out who these clues belonged to:

Clue	Belonged to	Date

I can put the clues into chronological order:

Clue	Date

Find out what **chronological** means and write it in your history glossary.

True or false?

My true or false quiz is about …

	True	False
1 _____	☐	☐
2 _____	☐	☐
3 _____	☐	☐
4 _____	☐	☐
5 _____	☐	☐
6 _____	☐	☐
7 _____	☐	☐
8 _____	☐	☐

When you've finished writing your quiz, give it to a friend. If your friend gets stuck, write some clues in these boxes.

Clue for question ⬭

Clue for question ⬭

Clue for question ⬭

Planning my questionnaire

I am trying to find out about …

I will interview …

The interview will take place at …

I might ask these questions:

Discuss your ideas with a friend before using 'My Questionnaire' sheet. Write any new ideas here:

My questionnaire

Interviewer's name:

Interviewee's name:

Questions

Answers

Signed _____

Signed _____

Planning our work together

We can brainstorm our ideas.

Name

Name

Name

Name

This is what _____ will do.

This is what _____ will do.

This is what _____ will do.

This is what _____ will do.

Our ideas for presenting our work:

Working together

We have been finding out about …

This is what _____ found out …

This is what _____ found out …

This is what _____ found out …

This is what _____ found out …

Write down the main points. Use them to help you decide what to include in your project.

We used these sources:

This is how we have decided to present our work:

How to be Brilliant at Recording in History

What would I do?

Event:

This is what has happened:

This is what I would do:

I would do this because …

These may be the results of what I did …

My sources were …

The best source was …

Building – my job sheet

I am planning to build …

I will need:

The building will look like this:

You can draw or describe your building.

Workers

Materials

Tools

Supplies (for the workers)

How to be Brilliant at Recording in History

My history glossary

1　Use this page to write down any historical words you don't understand.

2　When you've got time, try to find out what they mean.

3　When you understand a word, try to use it in your work.

Word	Meaning

How to be Brilliant at Recording in History

Self assessment

I've been finding out about …

This is what I liked best …

This is what I liked least …

This is what I did best …

This is what I could do better …

These are the skills I used …

This is what _____ thinks …

Ask a friend to write in this box.

Signed _____ Date _____

How to be Brilliant at Recording in History

My last history lesson

This is my last history lesson in Year _____ .

This is what I can remember …

My top 10

This is my top 10. The work I liked best is number 1.

1
2
3
4
5
6
7
8
9
10

If you can't remember 10 things, just write down the ones you can.